PRINCE

by GORDON MATTHEWS

JULIAN MESSNER  NEW YORK

Copyright © 1985 by Gordon R. Matthews
and 2M Communications Ltd.
All rights reserved
including the right of reproduction
in whole or in part in any form.
Published by Julian Messner,
A Division of Simon & Schuster, Inc.
Simon & Schuster Building
Rockefeller Center
1230 Avenue of the Americas
New York, New York 10020

JULIAN MESSNER and colophon are
trademarks of Simon & Schuster, Inc.
Also available in Wanderer Paperback Edition.
Manufactured in the United States of America

10 9 8 7 6 5 4 3 2 1

Designed by Irving Perkins Associates

Library of Congress Cataloging in Publication Data

Matthews, Gordon (Gordon R.)
    Prince.

    Discography: p.
    Summary: A biography of the rock singer, musician, and composer from Minneapolis, Prince, who became even more famous in the movie "Purple Rain."
    1. Prince. 2. Rock musicians—Biography—Juvenile literature. [1. Prince. 2. Musicians. 3. Rock music]
    I. Title.
ML3930.P756M37   1985   784.5'4'00924 [92]   84-27069
ISBN 0-671-55480-8 (lib. bdg.)
ISBN 0-671-55477-8 (pbk.)

CONTENTS

INTRODUCTION

MINNEAPOLIS, MINNESOTA, 1984
A small neighborhood record store

"Hey, you're not going to believe who was just in here."

"Who?"

"Prince!"

"You're kidding!"

"No, he didn't even have a bodyguard with him, just some girl I didn't recognize."

"Wow! What did he buy?"

"Let's see. *Hey Jude* by the Beatles, *Girl At Her Volcano* by Rickie Lee Jones, *The Jackie Wilson Story*, Alan Vega, and the new album by the Call."

"Did he say anything?"

"Not a word; and I gave him a discount, too. My hands were shaking!"

"I saw him in the Oak Grove grocery the other day. He bought fruit juice and tea."

So goes a typical exchange between two music fans on a typical day in Minneapolis, Minnesota. Someone saw Prince's purple limousine cruising down the street; someone saw Prince checking out a band at the club First Avenue; someone saw Prince at 2 A.M. sitting by himself in Froggy's Diner sipping on a soda.

Minneapolis is Prince's home town, and in 1984 he is musical king of that northern city. Not since Elvis Presley took over Memphis, Tennessee, has a rock-and-roller been so completely identified with one place. It was not always this way. Ten years ago, Prince was sleeping in a basement in Minneapolis, trying to avoid the centipedes.

The story of Prince is the story of a boy determined to succeed. Through sheer force of will and God-given talent, he has made it to the top. Along the way friends were made and lost, love was hard to find, and a lesson or two was learned the hard way. In the end the music world discovered a new hero.

Since its release in June of 1984, Prince's album *Purple Rain* has sold more than eight million copies. The movie of the same name is a huge success. If 1983 was the year of *Thriller* and Michael Jackson, then 1984 is certainly the year of *Purple Rain* and Prince.

THE EARLY YEARS

PRINCE WAS born Prince Roger Nelson on June 7, 1958, in south Minneapolis. His parents, Mattie and John Nelson, named him after a band they had both been in called the Prince Roger Trio; Mattie was a singer and John a pianist. When the two married, Mattie quit the band but John continued to play—working as a plaster molder to make ends meet.

Prince is not the most common name for a child. "I took a lot of kidding over it," admitted Prince in 1981. "The kids all called me Prince Charming and prince-this and prince-that. It's not the most masculine name in the world."

Prince remembers seeing his father perform when he was about five years old. That experience started the dream and made his decision: he would become a musician. "We were supposed to stay in the car, but I snuck out and went into the bar. He was up on the stage and it was amazing. I remembered thinking, these people think my Dad is great. I wanted to be part of that."

According to the writer Jon Bream, Prince wrote his

first song around the same time by banging two rocks together. Even from an early age Prince knew a song had to have a beat!

His mother can remember his musical talents taking form at an early age. "When he was three or four," she told Bream, "he'd jump on the radio, the organ, any type of instrument there was . . . he could hear music even from a very early age."

Prince's memories of his childhood are not very happy. His parents fought a lot, and by the time he was seven his father had moved out of the house. They were eventually divorced. The only thing he left behind was his piano—it was too big to take along. Prince had never been allowed to play the piano when his father lived at home because John Nelson did not think it was a toy for children to bang on. With his father gone, Prince started teaching himself to play. First he learned the theme songs from T.V. shows like "The Man From U.N.C.L.E." and "Batman." He took one piano lesson but quit because he did not want to be told what and how to play. It was a stubborn streak he inherited from his father.

When Prince was ten his mother married a man named Haywood Baker. Prince did not get along with his step-father. Baker had two children of his own and, according to Prince, had trouble showing his affection. "He would bring us a lot of presents all the time, rather than sit down and talk with us and give us companionship. I got real bitter because of that," Prince told Barbara Graustark in *Musician* magazine. "I would say all the things that I disliked about him, rather than tell him what I really needed." Prince now regrets that he was not able to express his needs to his stepfather. The price paid was a stormy relationship.

His stepfather was very strict. Prince recalls being grounded to his room for an entire week. There was nothing in the room but his bed and his father's old pi-

ano—needless to say, Prince got to practice quite a lot.

As Prince grew into his teens, the battles with his step-father finally drove him out of the house. He ran away to live with his real father. Prince always wanted to be close to his dad, but it was hard for them. His father worked two jobs: a day job and his "real" job, playing piano in bars at night. Father and son did not see eye-to-eye on a lot of things; Prince wanted more freedom than his father saw fit to give him.

Soon he was packing his bags once more, this time to live with an aunt. Prince's father had seen the musician inside his son and bought him a guitar, and his endless practicing drove his aunt up the wall. It was obvious, however, that he was on the way to becoming a talented instrumentalist. He would eventually claim to play over twenty different instruments.

Those years were troubled times for Prince. It has been said that, throughout his youth, he lived in as many as fourteen different places. Without a stable home Prince grew very insecure, withdrawn, and quiet; he also learned to distrust strangers. It was only through the out-let of his music that he could channel his troubles and frustrations in a positive way: music became his salvation.

LIFE IN THE BASEMENT

PRINCE STARTED in his first group as a way to compete with his older stepbrother, Duane. Prince and Duane were both in the same grade at school. "My older brother was the basketball and football star," Prince told Robert Hillburn of the *Los Angeles Times*. "He always had all the girls around him and stuff like that. I think I must have been on a jealousy trip, because I got out of sports . . . I wasn't bad at basketball, but my brother was better and he wouldn't let me forget it. There were other guys like that too.

"I just wanted to do something else and when I did get a band, the first thing you did was bring it to school and play the homecoming dance and say, 'Look at that.' It was something *they* couldn't do."

Prince formed his first band, Grand Central, with his best friend André Anderson. The two had met in junior high school and had become best friends. They did not know it then, but as small children they had played together. By a rather strange coincidence, their fathers had been in the same music group years earlier. They discovered the fact one day when André came over to visit

14

Prince and saw a picture of John Nelson's old band. "That looks like my dad!" shouted André when he spotted the picture.

André had been a bit of a troublemaker and Prince's mother and stepfather had not liked him. "Prince's parents did not want me around him," admits André. "They would ground him just so he would stay away from me."

Prince ended up on André's doorstep when he became too much for his aunt to handle. André's mother Bernadette took him in, letting him share André's room.

"When we were little, about thirteen," Andre told *Rock and Soul,* "we had this room with really small beds. We were really separate people, and wanted to divide the room to prove it. So I took a piece of tape and put it in the center of the room and up the walls. My side was packed with junk. . . . Prince's side was immaculate. His clothes were always hung up or folded. He even made his bed every day!"

Eventually Prince decided it would be easier if he

moved into the basement of the house, which would give him some privacy. Finally he had his own space, away from parental interference and discipline, a private world of his own. Prince felt more at home than he ever had. "My brain was free of everything," he said years later, "I didn't have anything to worry about. I knew it was okay to explore whatever I wanted down there in the basement because things weren't forbidden anymore. That's when I realized that music could express what you were feeling, and it started coming out in my songs. . . ."

The Anderson basement became Prince's laboratory. There he could explore and create in the world of music with complete freedom and abandon. It was there that he and André put together their first band, Grand Central. Prince played lead guitar, André played bass, André's sister played keyboards, and Prince's cousin Charles Smith was the drummer. At different periods in the band's development, Terry Jackson and William Daughty played percussion.

Even though they were very young, the band was considered to be quite good. André's mother did not even mind all the pounding and raucous noises that vibrated through the floorboards. The way she looked at it was, as long as the kids stayed in school and got good grades they could do whatever they wanted to in their spare time. If things got a little noisy around the house, at least she knew where her kids were—keeping the band going would keep her kids out of trouble.

On Saturdays the band would set up on the Anderson front lawn and perform for the neighborhood until the police came to make them stop. They played anywhere and everywhere they could. One of their biggest fans was John Nelson, Prince's dad, who would come and photograph the band. Despite their difficulties in communicating with each other in words, his father showed support in his own special way.

Grand Central was a Top 40 band. They played songs

by Sly and the Family Stone, Larry Graham, and even some Michael Jackson. They played black music but they were listening to music by white artists as well. Because the black population of Minneapolis is small, Prince and his band had to play all sorts of music to make their audiences dance. The frustrating thing was that it was not his own music.

"I hated 'Top 40,'" Prince said years later. "Everybody in the band hated it. It was what was holding us back. And we were trying to escape it. But we had to do it to make enough money to make demo tapes."

Demo tapes, short for demonstration tapes, are recordings an artist makes in a studio to audition for record companies. Record companies have scouts called A & R men or women (A & R stands for artists and repertoire). Their job is to find new artists and new songs that they think will be hits. They do this by listening to many demo tapes.

Before Grand Central recorded any demo material, they changed their name to Champagne and got a new drummer, Morris Day. Morris sat in with the band one day and it was obvious that he was a better drummer than Prince's cousin Charles. Morris was in, Charles was out, and the band had a new manager: Morris Day's mother.

When Prince graduated from high school he suddenly felt alone and adrift. The band was not making lots of money and he certainly did not want to work in a non-musical, ordinary job. Prince retreated deep into his basement and started writing furiously. He wanted to make it and he knew the only way to do that was to come up with hit songs. Songs that he wrote himself.

"I was writing like three or four songs a day. And they were all really long," remembers Prince.

Armed with Prince's new original material, Champagne marched into Moon Sound studio to do the demos they hoped would land them a recording contract. The sessions were recorded by the owner of the studio, Chris

Moon. He was not very impressed with the band or the songs, but he was impressed with Prince.

Moon suggested the two try to collaborate on some songwriting. Moon had written lyrics for a song he wanted to call "Soft and Wet." He thought Prince would be the right person to set them to music. In exchange for helping him write the song, Moon let Prince have free run of the studio. "He'd stay the weekend, sleep on the studio floor," Moon told Debbie Miller of *Rolling Stone*. "I wrote down directions on how to operate the equipment, so he'd just follow the little chart—you know, press this button to record and this button to play back. That's when he learned to operate studio equipment. Pretty soon I could sit back and do the listening."

Because he had learned to play so many instruments over the years, Prince was able to play all the parts himself, recording track by track until he had a finished demo tape. He was proud of his work but his band was a little put out that he recorded without them. Already Prince was proving to be his own man, willing and able to do things himself.

Anxious to have something happen with his career, he decided he should go to New York City where many large record companies had their headquarters. Prince tried to convince the rest of the band that they should move there, but they were opposed to taking such a giant step; even his best buddy André was not ready to take the plunge.

"I don't think they liked the idea of me manipulating the band so much. I was trying to get us to do something different . . . it was always me against them."

So once again Prince was alone and packing his bags to move on. Hurt and disappointed that André and the rest of the band would not follow his lead, Prince vowed to make it on his own. He was going to New York City.

NEW YORK AND CALIFORNIA

LUCKILY FOR Prince, his older stepsister Sharon, a stepsister on his father's side, was already living in Manhattan. Not only did she take him in when he showed up on her doorstep, she promised to help him get a record deal.

Sharon had a friend who managed a group and was planning to meet with a record producer about a deal. Sharon got herself invited along—and brought her little brother with her. The record producer was a French woman named Danielle Mauroy. She did not think much of Sharon's friend's tape. It was then that Sharon decided to make her move. She told Danielle that her brother was a wonderful singer–songwriter, so Danielle asked Prince if he would sing for her. What an opportunity—but he was too scared. He hadn't realized things would happen quite like this. After some gentle persuasion Prince agreed to sing. The lights were turned down, and he belted out a song he had just written, singing a capella. The song was called "Baby" and it eventually appeared on his first album.

"Baby what are we gonna do," wailed Prince in his beautiful high falsetto. He sounded good, even to himself. The song was not even finished when Prince sang it that day, and he had to hum and make up lyrics on the spot to fill it out.

Danielle Mauroy was impressed and eager to work with this new young artist, and invited him over to her apartment to hear more of his material. Prince was ecstatic; he thought he was really on his way at last. But things just don't happen that quickly.

Danielle did not like any of the songs Prince played for her except "Baby". Still, Prince was eager to make a record and Danielle told him that he would, but he could only sing on the record; he couldn't play. For a multi-instrumentalist like Prince this did not sit well at all.

Furthermore, Danielle wanted to buy the publishing rights to Prince's songs for a small amount of money. Knowing that she didn't like most of his material, it seemed like a bad idea to Prince. But Sharon was all for selling the rights. Prince might have gone along with it if he hadn't gotten an urgent phone call from Minneapolis. His friend Chris Moon had played the Prince demos for a manager in Minneapolis named Owen Husney. Husney, like Danielle, was not all that impressed by the songs, but when Chris Moon told him that Prince had played all the instruments on the demo, Husney realized he could have a real star in the making. Husney and Moon tracked Prince down in New York. "When I finally reached him on the phone, he was thinking of signing all his music publishing away to this lady from Paris," Husney told Steven Ivory. Just in time, he convinced Prince to come back to Minneapolis. Prince told Danielle and other New York record companies which were showing interest in the young artist that he had decided to go back to school.

Perhaps what convinced Prince to return to Minneapolis more than anything else was Husney's insis-

tence that no one but Prince himself should produce his work. Prince also sensed that he needed strong management in order to get a good record deal. Husney's encouragement sealed the deal.

"I went back to Minneapolis and back to André's basement—I could deal with the centipedes and poverty better because I knew that I could make it, I'd proven it to myself and that's what really mattered."

André Anderson, who would soon be going by the name André Cymone, was surprised but glad to see his old friend. Prince was welcomed back to the Anderson home. Champagne had fizzled out as a group since Prince had left town; without his leadership and songwriting power the band had not been able to carry on. Though André had the confidence to work on his own projects, he was more than happy to work with Prince again.

Even more exciting for Prince was the news that Owen Husney was willing to bankroll him in return for the right to manage the boy. Husney put Prince on a $50-a-week salary and got him his own apartment. This was the best yet—finally Prince didn't have to worry about getting kicked out of a place, because this place was his own. The only thing he had to watch out for were the numerous complaints from his neighbors for playing his guitar loud!

Prince began working in Chris Moon's studio again, re-recording his demo, making it better. When he was done he had improved versions of "Soft and Wet," "Baby," and a third song, "Make It Through the Storm." Husney also bought Prince a synthesizer, an instrument he quickly mastered. It would become an important part of his sound.

With the finished demo tape, Husney planned a strategy to put the artist across to the record labels. He put together expensive press kits, featuring a long series of photographs of the young artist. Each photo had a different pose of him holding a different instrument. On the last page was a picture of Prince with all the instruments around him. The idea was to make an impression of Prince as a budding young genius much like Stevie Wonder. The press kit also said Prince was two years younger than he really was. That way he would seem like a real child prodigy.

With the tape and the impressive press package under his arm and Prince by his side, Owen Husney went to California to pitch Prince to the record labels. First he would show record executives the press kit. Then he would play them the tape of "Soft and Wet" and "Baby." If they wanted to hear more, he had "Make It Through the Storm" waiting in his pocket. If, after the showing, the executive was interested, Husney would bring in Prince himself.

Prince lacked confidence talking to businessmen and preferred to have his manager speak for him. Warner Brothers was the first company to show some interest, but before too long other labels were jumping on the bandwagon. A & M and CBS also wanted the young artist. The problem was that the labels did not think such a young man could produce himself. But Husney was adamant. The label that would get Prince would let him produce.

Chris Butler, the songwriter of the Waitresses' hit "I Know What Boys Like," remembers meeting Prince around that time in Warner Brothers recording studio. "I was in Studio B with my band Tin Huey," remembers Chris. "Then one day this guy named Prince was in Studio A recording something. It was all very secretive. I met Prince out by the coffee machine. All the heavies from the label were there and they introduced me to him. . . . We were both from the Midwest so I made some small talk about that but Prince didn't react at all. I remember him being a little guy with a huge afro. It wasn't like he was acting cool. He just seemed scared."

Husney suggested to Warner Brothers that they devise a test for Prince: put Prince in the studio and let the top executives at the company watch. Husney figured once they saw how well Prince knew his way around the studio they would agree to let him produce himself. He didn't tell Prince who the guys standing around the studio were the day of the test: he did not want to make Prince unduly nervous. Husney's strategy worked. Once the label people saw Prince work, they were convinced; Prince would be allowed to produce himself.

Prince returned to Minneapolis a happy man. Originally he had planned to record the album there at Chris Moon's studio, but the engineer on the session insisted that they needed the modern equipment found only in the West Coast studios. It was decided that they would record at the Record Plant in Sausalito where two of Prince's heroes, Carlos Santana and Sly Stone, had worked. Prince also convinced André to come with him. André remembers telling Prince, "Look . . . I'll play with you until you get your thing established to where you want it. But then I'm going to split and go back to what I was doing before."

So André went along with Prince to California to make Prince's first album. They set up in an apartment in the San Francisco area with Owen and his wife Britt.

"I was a physical wreck when I finished the record," Prince told Barbara Graustark. "It took me five months to do the first one. I'm proud of it, in the sense that it's mistake-free, and it's perfect."

Prince's first record went way over budget. It cost more than $170,000 to make. Artists making their first record often try to make everything "too perfect:" they think every note has to be right in place, and they lose spontaneity and spirit in the process. Prince was so concerned with making a great record that he went overboard. Because he did almost everyting himself, the process was slow and time consuming.

That first album, *For You* (1978), was not a bad record, but compared to records he would later make it sounds slick and unadventurous. The album included "Baby" and "Soft and Wet." Other stand-out songs were the title cut and the slow jazzy ballad, "Crazy You." The most interesting song on the record was "I'm Yours." It broke the mold a little with Prince playing some wild lead guitar.

For You sold pretty well for a first release, around 100,000 copies, but Prince would have to do a lot better than that if Warner Brothers were going to make any money—and retain him.

Warner's designed a campaign to promote the record and the artist as a young genius à la Stevie Wonder. "Who is Prince?" said the full-page ads in *Billboard*. The cover of the album was blurry and out of focus. You could barely make out what Prince looked like, just those big watery eyes and the shining edge of an afro. The back cover had

just a list of the songs and in big letters "Produced, Arranged, Composed, and Performed by Prince." Chris Moon received credit for co-writing "Soft and Wet."

Prince played his first official date as a solo artist in January of 1978 at the Capri Lounge in Minneapolis. The place held about 500, and 300 people showed up to check out the local boy with the record contract. It was an odd show because Prince did not use a full band. Instead of a drummer he used a rhythm machine. Keyboard and bass parts were on tape. Prince took the stage with two other men playing guitar.

Eventually Prince did put a band together: André Cymone played bass, Dez Dickerson played guitar, Bobby Z. was the new drummer, and a girl named Gale Chapman would play keyboards. Prince did some dates as the opening band for Rick James, but being an opening act was not to his liking. It has been said that Prince refused to talk to James on the tour and did everything he could to upstage the headliner.

Not only did Prince not like opening for other performers, he didn't like all the politics that went along with

Prince with Dez Dickerson

promoting a record. Doing interviews was very difficult for him. Sometimes he would just sit there muttering one-word responses. He didn't like all the people patting him on the back telling him how great he was when he felt they had never even heard his record.

He knew the only way to get beyond all that was to make a hit record, and when he went back into the studio that's just what he did.

His next album, called simply *Prince*, showed that he had learned a lot in the last year. The record was far more relaxed and in the groove. Some of the songs were more experimental like "When We're Dancing Close and Slow." "Bambi" was the closest thing Prince had done to hard rock. But most important were the hits, the long funk groove number "Sexy Dancer," and the biggest hit of all, "I Wanna Be Your Lover," a slice of modern dance pop that raced up the charts. It helped the second album reach gold status (sales of over 500,000 copies).

Prince was on his way, but he was still not satisfied with the records he was making. "The second album was pretty contrived," he told Robert Hillburn. "I had put myself in the hole with the first record because I spent a lot of money to make it. I wanted to remedy that with the second album. I wanted a 'hit' album. It was for radio rather than for me, and it got a lot of people interested in my music. But it wasn't the kind of audience I really want. *They* only came around to check you out when you had another hit. *They* won't come to see you when you change directions and try something new. *That's* the kind of audience I wanted."

Indeed, many people who saw Prince because they bought his second album came away confused. Prince was different than what they expected, to say the least. Prince's outlandish stage garb surprised and shocked some people. Trench coats and bikini briefs on a guy were just too weird.

Kelly Tucker, a reporter for the *Times–Picayune* in New Orleans, described the audience response to a Prince show in December of 1979: "Throughout the show Prince did not receive nearly as much response as he deserved. When he walked off stage at the end of the set, the audience hardly made a sound. It was only after his embarrassed manager walked to the microphone and asked the crowd if they wanted more that sparse applause and shouts began."

When the reporter asked members of the audience why they didn't like the show they gave responses like, "He should have stayed in L.A. We don't like freaks in New Orleans," to "We were expecting a guy who looked more like a man; he dressed too weird."

Prince explained to *New York Rocker's* Andy Schwartz why he wore so little clothing on stage. "I've gotten a lot of criticism from outsiders, but once they see the show they understand why I wear what I wear. The show's real athletic and we run around a lot, and I have to be real comfortable. The decision was left up to me, and when I thought about what I was most comfortable in, it's what I sleep in . . . I just can't stand clothes."

If you look at the cover of the second Prince album he certainly meant what he said. By 1979 Prince had straightened his hair and, with the exception of an earring, it appears that he is wearing nothing at all—of course the cover shot is only from the chest up. On the back is a picture of Prince riding a horse with wings.

Prince wanted an image that was totally original, that would make people look up and say "Wow I've never seen anything like him before!"

Prince returned to Minneapolis after the release of his second album for a home town show. Even though he had a hit record he was hard pressed to sell out the local concert theater. His concert at the Orpheum only drew about a thousand people, in a theatre that held 2,300. It must have bothered Prince and made him think harder about what he had to do to make it really big.

Prince began hanging out at a nightclub in Minneapolis called Sam's, more recently named First Avenue. The club was a new wave club where patrons dressed up in the latest punk fashion styles, leather jackets, funny haircuts and make-up. The music they danced to was new and different and it made sense to Prince. Bands like the B–52's, Devo, and Talking Heads had them shaking on the dance floor to a new and different sound. There was something fresh and urgent about the new music and it appealed to Prince.

THE NEW SOUND

PRINCE WANTED to make music that would reach all types of people. He wanted to make music that went beyond the categories—black, white, punk or disco—something that he could truly call his own. The album that would bring all these styles together was called *Dirty Mind* and would cause Prince to lose some fans and gain others. On the cover was a black-and-white photo of Prince wearing his now famous purple trenchcoat. In the lapel of the jacket was a button that said "Rude Boy," and around his neck was a kerchief. On his legs were thigh-high legwarmers, and the only other thing he had on was black bikini underwear. The music inside was just as interesting.

The record really rocked. It had a fresh sound like nothing anyone had heard before. You could dance to its somewhat disco-ish beat, but there were guitar solos and angry vocals, so it was also rock. Prince had successfully joined two types of music that people had considered separate.

"It started out as a demo tape," Prince explained, "and

I didn't take a lot of time with it. But by the time I finished, the anger came through.

"I got a new guitar before I made the record, and I started to play more on it, rather than just filling up space with other instruments," he told Dennis Wilen of the *Los Angeles Herald-Examiner*. *Dirty Mind* was actually recorded as a series of demos that Prince had made for his own pleasure. But then he played them for his new manager, Steve Fargnoli.

Prince recorded the demos in Minneapolis in a small sixteen-track studio, and was trying to decide on the best songs to take to California and record. His manager thought they sounded fine the way they were because they were so fresh and raw. "I thought *Dirty Mind* was an album that deserved to be made," Steve Fargnoli told Robert Hillburn. "But Warner Brothers understandably, didn't know how to react. The last record had sold almost a million, and they expected something with the same sound. They were very negative at first—about the music and the cover—but they eventually got behind it.

"They said . . . 'it's not like your last album at all,' and Prince countered by saying, 'But it's more like me.' After the record was released Prince told the press, 'I'm not going to bow down to the establishment to make records like they want me to make. That's why there's a sales slump . . . There used to be an attitude where everybody tried to be as different as they could be. Now, it's rather dead. I'm trying to put some life back into the industry, at least for me.'"

Dirty Mind only sold about half as well as his second album had, but what was important was the fact that people were buying his record even though it did not have a big radio hit on it. People were taking notice of Prince as a performer and songwriter rather than as a name attached to this week's big hit song. People were curious—who was this guy who was making this weird new music and why did he wear such bizarre outfits?

Because radio was not playing the *Dirty Mind* album, Prince decided that he should talk to the press to help get his message across. Prince probably did more interviews at this time than at any other point in his career; he still did not enjoy the experience.

He told Dennis Hunt of the *Los Angeles Times*: "I'm really shy when I meet someone for the first time. You see I like to listen. I think other people are more interesting than I am. An interview means I have to do all the talking.

"My first two albums were self-explanatory but this one isn't," he said. "People have to understand me better to understand the album. Through the interviews people may be able to find out where I'm coming from and maybe get into the album a little easier."

"It would take crowbar to pry a quote out of him," said a reporter who interviewed him at the time. "He was like a fragile woodland creature: when he hears the steps of mankind approaching he beats a hasty retreat into his private world. He knows what his strengths are and he knows he does not come across well in a one-on-one encounter."

The place that Prince did feel comfortable was on stage. His show had been sharpened to perfection, and his band knocked out audiences wherever they went.

"We're just going to keep playing until enough people hear us," Prince told *New York Rocker*. "I don't care if it sells so much as I want people to understand it, to give them the chance to see and hear it. Just from talking to kids on the street and people I meet, a lot of people didn't even know the songs, you could tell 'cause they weren't singing along, but we had their attention. They never turned away. That means more to me than running out and buying. I just want them to listen, that's all."

"People who come to our shows are really into us," he told the *Daily News* before a show at the Flipper disco in Los Angeles. "And if this one's like most of the rest of this tour, it will be a half black and half white audience."

Prince and his band had successfully drawn a racially mixed audience, something that hadn't been done in almost ten years, when both blacks and whites would go to shows by artists like Sly and the Family Stone or Jimi Hendrix. With the advent of disco, blacks and whites seemed to move in separate musical directions. Prince was bringing the two groups back into the same clubs and concert halls.

Perhaps Prince was able to do this because he himself did not consider himself black or white. His parents were a mixture of different races and the music he grew up listening to was by both black and white artists. His band was also racially and sexually mixed.

Prince was writing and recording more than ever, but was not due to release an album for a while. He didn't want to sit on his new material, yet didn't have an outlet for it all. When along came a mysterous character named Jamie Starr.

Mr. Starr had been given credit for engineering the *Dirty Mind* album in 1980. Soon after, his name would appear on other records as well. In April of 1981, the first album by a new Minneapolis group called The Time was released. The front person for The Time was Morris Day, the drummer for Prince's high school band Champagne. As vocalist for The Time, Morris was something to behold: proud and vain, yet terribly funny. He was the perfect vehicle for songs like "Cool" and "Get It Up." The Time seemed the picture of elegance and class, dressing in sharkskin suits and ties.

"We're saying be concerned with your appearance," Morris told Skippy Lawson, "and don't be afraid to watch the way you walk and talk or look in the mirror to check your hair out. Cool is self respect." As if to prove his point, in part of The Time's act, a member of the band acted as Morris's valet, holding up a mirror for the singer on stage in the middle of the show!

The Time album was produced by Morris Day and Jamie Starr. The new question became, who is this Jamie Starr, anyway? Once reporters started snooping around they realized that Jamie Starr was a pseudonym for Prince himself. "I am not Jamie Starr," Prince would tell the press. According to sources close to Prince, Jamie Starr is a way for Prince to gain some distance on himself. So that he can be both Prince the performer and the producer. Since people discovered his secret, Jamie Starr is now only referred to as the Starr Company.

The Time was a little more mainstream than the stuff Prince had given the world on *Dirty Mind* and it sold quite well. This way Prince could have his cake and eat it too. If he could not get hits with his own records, he would write and produce others through The Time, and still continue to make the records he wanted under his own name.

Prince was just bursting with ideas and new songs. He wanted to do it all and to do it his way. This evolved into a problem for the other people in his band, who were also creative; Prince had set up a talented pool of musicians to work with. Over the next few years more than one would chafe under the tight rein Prince held them with.

The first to leave was Prince's oldest comrade, André Cymone. André claims the split was caused because he was the first to be interested in working with The Time. "I put the whole thing together," Cymone told *Rock and Soul* magazine. "I got him involved. I was going to write some of the songs. All of a sudden, Prince decided he wanted everything his way. He didn't want my name to be mentioned . . . either I was going to get something out of it, or it would be best for me to split and start making a name for myself."

Prince did not want to see André go. They had been as close as brothers, but André could no longer play second fiddle to him. André and Prince are not on the best of terms today, but André hopes they will someday work together again. "I still love Prince like a brother," he admits. Now André is busy with his own career. He has put out two albums under his own name and has produced many different people, including Evelyn Champagne King.

Prince's next album was sure to raise controversy and that was the name of the album, *Controversy*. The album commented on all the things people, and especially the press, had been saying about Prince. The cover showed Prince wearing the same trenchcoat and "Rude Boy" button that he had worn on the cover of *Dirty Mind*. In contrast to the legwarmers and underwear underneath the jacket on the cover of *Dirty Mind,* though, Prince was now sporting a tuxedo shirt and tie. Was he cleaning up his act?

Prince seemed to be reaching outside himself for inspiration on *Controversy*. "Ronnie Talk to Russia" was a plea to President Reagan to sit down with the Russians and work out an arms limitation agreement "before they blow up the world." The song had a gospel feel that would be perfect for a frenzied Baptist church service. "Annie Christian" makes a strong statement about gun control.

Meanwhile, the Prince cult continued to grow, though he was still far from being a major star. Radio stations still were not playing his music with much regularity and if it weren't for the praise of critics and his fantastic live shows, Prince might not have continued to grow.

He was, however, a major star in his home town. The club First Avenue in Minneapolis became a kind of clubhouse for Prince. He would show up and jam with various musicians that performed there, and he would book secret shows there where local fans could gather to pay homage to their new hero.

Many people agree that one of the best shows Prince has ever played was at First Avenue in March of 1982. Prince felt relaxed performing in the Minneapolis club. This was his home and he was the conquering hero. He kicked out the jams and grooved that night. "This ain't a concert . . . this is a dance!" he shouted to his faithful followers, and everybody got down and shook it for all they were worth.

One reason Prince felt so good was the fact that he had fallen in love. The lucky lady was the beautiful Denise Mathews, otherwise known as Vanity. Vanity was a model from Ontario, Canada, who had made a couple of films in her native country and was also trying to break in as a singer-songwriter. Prince took one look at her and decided he could fall in love and make Vanity a star in the process. Soon Vanity was leading her own group, a female trio called Vanity Six, had a hit album—produced by Jamie Starr, of course—and was pictured with Prince on the cover of *Rolling Stone* magazine.

In 1983 Prince would take The Time (who had released their second hit album), Vanity Six, and his own band on a long and grueling national tour. Vanity Six opened with a short set, followed by the steamy funky showmanship of The Time. This was all a lead-in to the main event: Prince himself, who entered the stage by sliding down a fireman's pole.

The tour was a huge success. When the three groups tried to leave an arena in Columbus, Ohio, they were mobbed by fans. It took thirty-six policemen and security guards to get them out. At a local record store, 3,000 fans showed up for an autograph signing by Vanity Six and The Time. Meanwhile, The Time had upset the telephone company with their song "777—9311." People that happened to have that phone number around the country were being inundated with calls asking, "Hello, is Morris there?"

But the big news was that Prince was finally getting the air play he deserved with his brand new album *1999*. With the singles "*1999*" and "Little Red Corvette" played widely on the radio, the album went on to sell over three million copies. This was particularly surprising to Prince because *1999* is a double album.

"I didn't want to do a double album," Prince told Robert Hillburn in what would be his last interview to date, "but I just kept writing and I'm not one for editing

. . . I like a natural flow. I always compare songwriting to a girl walking through the door. You don't know what she's going to look like, but all of a sudden she's there."

1999 was by far Prince's best album up to that time. It covered all the bases. There were long dance tracks, experimental numbers, protest songs, ballads, hit singles, and real rockers. Prince had finally made it and he'd made it on his own terms. He no longer had to worry about doing interviews if he didn't want to, he no longer had to worry about reaching fans—he had them. Where was he to go from there?

Prince was not talking. As his tour bus traveled around the country, Prince sat off by himself, writing endlessly in a purple notebook.

AND THE RAIN
CAME DOWN

IN **1983** Michael Jackson's music was consistently played on the radio, with the release of his album *Thriller.* The big hits "Billie Jean" and "Beat It" had reached many new fans, so many that he sold more albums than any performer ever had before. "I don't care what they say about me anymore," Prince said in 1981. "Just don't compare me to Michael Jackson." But people were going to compare them whether Prince liked it or not. In some ways, the success of Michael Jackson fueled the success of Prince by creating a rivalry in the media much like that between the Beatles and the Rolling Stones in the 1960s. Because Michael was so remarkably popular there had to be an alternative to him who could be just as big. Prince was it. It's interesting that Michael and Prince have very little to say about one another.

A fact that many people forget is that Prince was first to get his videos on MTV, the popular music video cable station that many say brought the record industry out of its slump. MTV was accused for a long time of not playing videos by black artists, but they were playing Prince's

"Little Red Corvette" because it was such a great rock song. Prince may have opened the door for Michael, whose rock videos really went through the roof.

Prince knew that if he was going to make his mark, he would have to come up with something new and push himself to the limit. He would write and perform in his own movie.

Prince had been writing his ideas in a purple notebook for quite some time. He wanted to tell the story of his life in a fictional form. People would refer to it as "faction" or an "emotional biography." Although the facts were not exactly the same as his own life, the underlying emotional truths would be the same. Prince went to his management company and asked them what they thought. The idea intrigued them because, like Prince, they had never taken on such a challenge and they were ready for something new.

Writers were brought in to help Prince with the script. It was decided that Vanity would co-star, Morris Day would play a lovable villain, and Prince's band would play themselves.

Before the project even got off the ground, things began to fall apart, things that would ultimately affect the outcome of the movie. Dez Dickerson decided he wanted a solo career away from Prince; three members of The Time left the group because they wanted more freedom to work on outside projects; and Vanity herself decided things were not working out for her in Minneapolis.

Just as André Cymone had left because he wanted to run his own life, now others were following suit. Prince's kingdom was in a shambles and he had brought it upon himself. Taking responsibility for your own actions would become a central theme in his movie, along with the notion that you have to respect those around you while you follow your own personal dreams.

"I needed one person to love me, and he needed more," Vanity told *People* magazine. "I miss his humor. I always felt we'd be like Richard Burton and Elizabeth Taylor over the years. I can honestly say I love the kid."

Right now "the Kid," as he would be called in the movie, had to rebuild his kingdom. The Time had suffered real damage when keyboardist Jimmy Jam and bass player Terry Lewis left the band. They were followed by the other keyboardist Monte Moir. Prince replaced them with three new members: Terry Hubbard, Paul Peterson, and Mark Cardenas. It was certainly not the same band and at one point Prince tried to get Jam and Lewis to return to the band. By then, though, they were ready to be on their own. Since they left, Jam and Lewis have charted nine times with records they wrote and/or produced for the S.O.S. Band, Gladys Knight, Klymmax, and Cheryl Lynn.

How could Prince match the rocking fire of Dez Dickerson? Instead of trying, he took a new approach. From now on, Prince would do most of the lead guitar work and he'd find a good rhythm guitar player. Through keyboardist Lisa Coleman, Prince got Wendy Melvoin. Wendy and Lisa had known each other most of their lives. Their fathers were studio musicians who had played on records by the Beach Boys years before. Wendy fit right in. The band was now a fascinating mixture of characters.

"The idea of integration is important to Prince," Lisa Coleman told Kurt Loder of *Rolling Stone*. "It's just good fate that it's worked out as well as it has . . . he's chosen people in his band because of their musical abilities, but it does help to have two female musicians who are competent."

For the first time Prince gave his band a name: The Revolution.

Prince's biggest problem was to find a replacement for Vanity. How do you replace your girlfriend when she is also co-star of your movie?

A casting call went out across the country and 700 young women responded. Prince found his new co-star in a nineteen-year-old Hispanic-American girl named Patricia Kotero—soon to be re-named Apollonia.

Apollonia was discovered in Los Angeles where she had been working as a model and actress. When Prince met her he asked about her experience and if she believed in God. Prince has a deep commitment to God—his band prays together before every show and he has given special thanks to God on each of his album jackets.

Prince and Apollonia talked about all sorts of things that first day, then, after a ride in his limousine, he took her dancing at his favorite club, First Avenue.

Many people speculated that Apollonia was Prince's new girlfriend but when asked she would just say, "I don't kiss and tell." She did admit that she waited anxiously for the first kiss she would get from Prince. It would come in front of the cameras during the filming of the movie.

Prince worked hard rehearsing The Revolution, The Time and Apollonia 6. They not only practiced singing and playing, but took singing and acting lessons as well. Even Prince's bodyguard Chick would be in the movie.

The project got underway in the summer of 1983. Prince brought a mobile recording studio to First Avenue to record some new songs that he was playing as part of a benefit for the Minnesota Dance Theatre, the people who were teaching Prince and his entourage to dance. Among the songs performed were "I Would Die 4 U," "Baby I'm A Star," and the song that would become the theme song of his movie, "Purple Rain."

Originally the movie was going to be called "Dreams," but Prince was obsessed with the color purple. He had a purple car, a purple coat, a purple house, and a purple motorcycle. He might as well have a purple movie, too!

As the script was re-written under the watchful eye of Prince and director Albert Magnoli, the story began to

Apollonia pictured (center) with her band—Apollonia 6

take form. Magnoli described it to *Creem* magazine. "A girl comes into town to a club. She sweeps out of a cab in black. There's Prince — he's a dark figure. There's Morris—he's a light figure. There's the girl—she's a mystery."

Most of the action would take place at First Avenue. The club was closed for six weeks while the movie was shot. A call for extras went out and hundreds of hopefuls lined up in a suburban parking lot to try their luck at being part of Prince's movie. "Dress as you would to party with Prince," read the invitation to the extras. In the morning they auditioned men and in the afternoon, women.

Extras made $24 for a day's work plus a free lunch. Prince watched the applicants in the parking lot through the blinds of the hotel office. Once the extras were picked they were told not to speak to Prince on the set. If they did they would be fired immediately. Cameras were forbidden and the extras were also instructed not to speak to the press. Although only a few of them could be seen on the screen, the movie had 600 extras. The idea was to make First Avenue look like a packed night club even at seven o'clock in the morning when shooting began.

Although the music was pre-recorded, Prince insisted that the lip-synching be done with the music being played through the loudspeakers at concert volume. This way the audience of extras could feel they were at a real concert. The music was so loud that members of the technical crew bought $200 worth of sound protection devices.

In *Purple Rain* Prince plays the part of the Kid, a troubled but talented youth who is trying to make it with his rock group. Although he is not called Prince, everyone else in the movie uses his or her real name, except Prince's mother and father, who are played by Olga Karlotos and Clarence Williams III (who played Link on the popular 60s TV show, "The Mod Squad").

The Kid is less than a nice guy when the film starts. He refuses to listen to any of the songs that his band members, Lisa and Wendy, have written. He only wants to do his own material. Prince and Apollonia take a motorcycle ride together with the song "Take Me with U" playing in the background. They stop to walk by a lake, and he tells her he will only help her if she first passes an initiation. The initiation is to purify herself in the waters of Lake Minnetonka. Eager for the Kid's help, Apollonia strips down and hops into the lake. Then the Kid tells her she jumped into the wrong lake!

It becomes obvious that some of the Kid's problems stem from a troubled home life. His parents are constantly fighting and his father beats his mother. When the Kid tries to step in his father beats him too.

When Apollonia tells the Kid she is going to get help from Morris Day to start a group, he strikes her. It's a shocking moment in which the Kid realizes he is following in the footsteps of his father.

Suddenly everything crumbles for the Kid: his band might break up; the club owner tells him he is ready to dump the act because the Kid is just too weird; Apollonia leaves him; and, worst of all, his father shoots himself, ending up in the hospital in critical condition. The Kid's world is caving in on him and he takes off on his motorcycle, trying to sort his thoughts out while the song "When Doves Cry" plays in the background. Maybe he is just like his father, a troubled musician who tells him, "Never get married."

All through the movie the action is punctuated with song. When Apollonia first starts hanging out with Morris at the club Prince sings "The Beautiful Ones" from the stage, imploring his love to stay with him. "I want you baby," he screams at the end of the song as the camera zooms in on Apollonia's tear-stained face. Later, when he knows he has lost her, he sings the angry and nasty "Darling Nikki" to get back at her, and Apollonia storms out of the club. ("Nikki" was the name of the original heroine in the movie before Vanity was replaced by Apollonia.)

At the climactic finale, the Kid comes to grip with some of his problems. He dedicates a song to his father who is still in the hospital. The song is "Purple Rain." In the movie it is the song written by Wendy and Lisa that the Kid had earlier refused to play. The crowd is moved by it and sway back and forth, pointing heavenward as Prince plays the beautiful ballad. The Kid is called back to the stage for an encore and Apollonia is there waiting for him. He launches into "I Would Die 4U," a song inspired by something his father said to his mother whereby the Kid realized that, despite all their problems, his parents still love each other. There is a scene during the song of the Kid going to the hospital, where he sees his mother sleeping with her head on her husband's hospital bed. The movie closes with "Baby, I'm a Star," where the Kid pulls out all the stops and gets the whole place rocking, including the movie theater audience. Even Morris Day, who has been his rival all through the movie, is seen getting down and boogying.

If *Purple Rain* has a message, it is that one must rise above one's problems by guarding against selfishness and coming to terms with one's faults. Sometimes life deals us some tough blows but, like the Kid, we must go on living and rise above the sorrow and pain.

Along with all the Prince music, there were also songs by The Time, Dez Dickerson, and Apollonia 6. Perhaps most interesting was a piece written by Prince's father, John Nelson, a piano instrumental that Clarence Williams III, his screen father, is seen performing. The piece is simply called "Father's Song." There was too much music in the movie for one record, so the *Purple Rain* album was comprised completely of Prince songs. In the months following the movie, records would be released by The Time and Apollonia 6. Dez Dickerson is ready to release a record as well.

The first single released from *Purple Rain* was the single "When Doves Cry," which raced to the top of the pop charts within six weeks. When the album came out it too hit the number one spot—it was the first time a soundtrack album went to number one before the movie was even released!

The movie *Purple Rain* premiered in Los Angeles on July 26, 1984. It was a star-studded event attended by many of Hollywood's biggest celebrities. MTV broadcast the opening night party nationally, so fans got to watch for the stars who included Eddie Murphy, Lionel Richie, Stevie Nicks and Lindsay Buckingham of Fleetwood Mac, Pee Wee Herman, Steven Spielberg, Morgan Fairchild, and Little Richard.

Prince attends premiere of "Purple Rain."

The movie's cast was there as well. Morris Day arrived in a brightly colored Cadillac wearing a shiny white suit. Apollonia came in a Rolls Royce and was decked out in a beautiful purple evening gown. Of course the biggest star of all was Prince himself accompanied by his bodyguard Chick. Prince pulled up in his purple limousine, wearing his famous trenchcoat and carrying a purple flower. All the women who came to the party were given purple orchids, and everything at the after-show party was decorated in purple—there were even purple spotlights dancing across the sky.

After a performance by members of the Minneapolis Dance Theatre, Sheila E., Prince's latest musical find— also rumored to be his new girlfriend—took the stage and performed, followed by Prince and The Revolution, who played three songs.

Critics began raving about the movie, calling it the best rock-and-roll movie since the Beatles' first film, *A Hard Day's Night*. With great advance press and the number one album, the movie was primed for release. It opened across the country in close to a thousand theaters.

In one week the movie had already broken even, bringing in some seven million dollars at the box office.

During the month of July, Prince celebrated his twenty-sixth birthday at a special concert at First Avenue. Well wishers sang "Happy Birthday," and Prince and The Revolution played for over an hour and a half. That same month Prince flew to Dallas to check out the Jacksons' tour.

Although Michael has never acknowledged Prince as competition, the Jackson Brothers did see *Purple Rain* at a special screening. Meanwhile Prince was beating Michael and his brothers on the charts. Their *Victory* album and the single, "State of Shock," were selling at a far slower rate than Prince's album and single. To date, the *Purple Rain* album has sold over eight million copies, both "When Doves Cry" and "Let's Go Crazy" have gone to number one, and a third single of the song "Purple Rain" went Top 10. Prince was by far the biggest star of the summer and fall of 1984.

AFTER THE STORM

ONE OF the biggest surprises of *Purple Rain* was how good a comedic actor Morris Day turned out to be. As the Kid's rival, Morris was hilarious as he flaunted his ego and went through slapstick routines with his valet Jerome. The press especially singled out Morris' performance as being exemplary. It is not surprising that Morris has decided to leave the Prince empire to start out on his own.

The first hint of trouble came in July when Prince played with The Time in Minneapolis. Morris was nowhere to be seen. Then at the premiere party for *Purple Rain*, Morris and Prince did not speak to each other. Soon after there was talk of Morris Day working on a movie deal with Richard Pryor.

Once again it came down to a talented pupil wanting to get out from under his teacher. Prince owned the name The Time, and he wrote some of their early hits (according to *Rolling Stone*), if not a great deal of their material. Morris claims Prince was actually bugged by The Time's success. "It created a tension between us," he told *Rol-*

ling Stone. "There used to be some arguments before going on stage about things that I would do that were conflicting with things that Prince would do. I was told not to do certain things, certain dances."

Still Morris Day would not come out and say anything negative about Prince. After all, his part in *Purple Rain* had made him more popular than he had ever been before and he did owe much of his musical success to Prince for getting him started. "There's a lot of negative things I could say," he said recently. "But I don't want to see these things in print. I still consider the guy my friend."

According to sources in Minneapolis, The Time has now broken up for good. The remaining members are busy working on a new project, directed by Prince of course, called Family.

Prince is continually active. People that know say he has already recorded his next album and is working on the one after that. There are other projects as well.

With Sheila E.

"He's married to his work," Apollonia told *Us* magazine. "He's incredible to watch. I've never before been in awe of anyone but God. He has a safe full of unrecorded material—hits from now to eternity."

His latest lady, Sheila E., has a hit album on her hands with a top ten single "The Glamorous Life." Sheila Escovedo is now known as Sheila E., but Prince met her years ago when he was working on his first album. She is the daughter of Peter Escovedo, a Latin-jazz percussionist who had worked with Carlos Santana, one of Prince's earliest influences. Prince and Sheila have been writing songs together for years. Before she got her big break with Prince, she had toured as a back-up singer and percussionist for Lionel Richie, George Duke, and Marvin Gaye.

When Sheila recently played at the Ritz in New York City, Prince jumped on stage for an encore of "Erotic City," which also features Sheila E. on the flip side of the single "Let's Go Crazy." He then launched into an audience sing-along on "When Doves Cry."

Sheila won't talk about her supposed relationship with Prince. She told Kurt Loder, "We're just friends, but the public will assume what it wants.

"He's a good person," she added. "He's changed somewhat; he's really happy now."

Sheila E. was lucky to be chosen as the opening act for Prince's 1984 fall tour.

According to writer Jon Bream, Prince recently paid $450,000 for a huge warehouse in the suburbs of Minneapolis where he intends to build an ultramodern recording studio. There he will continue to write and record for himself and others.

Lately he has been letting other band members contribute more to the songwriting and arranging. Lisa and Wendy conducted a string section on three songs from *Purple Rain.* Sheila E., Apollonia 6 and members of The

Revolution have each contributed to the others' records as well.

"We play a lot together," Wendy Melvoin explained to *Musician* magazine about the way The Revolution works. "When we jam we'll get caught in a groove and, knowing each other's style so well, we can create a song. That's how a lot of stuff gets created and arranged . . . He hasn't tried to tame us down at all, and he's more willing to accept ideas from each of us."

Since the release of the movie, Prince has become more secretive. His purple house in the Minneapolis suburb of Chanhassen is surrounded by a tall black fence and re-mote control-operated gate. Sometimes he is seen riding around town in a BMW sportscar or his chauffur-driven purple limousine. He now travels almost always with one of his bodyguards.

Meanwhile, the tourists are flocking to First Avenue to have their pictures taken in front of the club or to check out the building across the street that they believe was Apollonia's hotel in the movie. Often Prince or The Time or other Minneapolis stars will do surprise shows. The promoter of First Avenue is a hard-working guy named Steve McClellan. Right now he is a little worried about some of the club's newly found notoriety. He is con-cerned that the tourists are not really interested in seeing the bands, and that they might drive the real music lovers away.

"My biggest fear is that the tourists won't listen to the music," said McClellan. "I have no intention of turning this place into a museum for Prince. Sure we could have wax figures of the band and we could have a glass case with the first glove Prince ever threw into the audience. But that's not why I got involved here. We'll continue to use this place to promote exciting entertainment and to help launch the stars of tomorrow."

Prince still comes by the place from time to time. He caught Tina Turner's show which opened with her rendi-

tion of Prince's "Let's Get Married." He was so inspired by a set by funkster George Clinton that he raced right home, wrote and recorded the song "Erotic City." When he has new material ready to be released he will often come down and have the dee jays at First Avenue give the material a test spin. Prince will then hop on the dance floor and see how his record rates.

He steers clear of the press now more than ever. His last interview was in 1982 in support of his album *1999*. It

was the first of four scheduled interviews, but after he did the first, he abruptly cancelled the rest. He has not made a public statement since.

In November of 1984, Prince began his first national tour at the Joe Louis Arena in Detroit. Seven separate shows at the stadium sold out more than 130,000 tickets.

Where does Prince go from here? He will probably make more movies; there has been talk of him starring in a movie about the life of the 1950s rocker Little Richard. He will undoubtedly start his own record label; and at the rate he is going it could be the next Motown. He already has the musicians and a sound he can call his own. It will be interesting to see where it leads.

"The most important thing is to be true to yourself, but I also like danger," he told Robert Hillburn in his last interview. "That's what is missing from pop music today. There's no excitement and mystery—people sneaking out and going to these forbidden concerts by Elvis Presley or Jimi Hendrix. I'm not saying I'm better than anybody else, but I don't feel like there are a lot of people out there telling the truth in their music."

Right now Prince is burning, filled with more songs and ideas than most artists have in a lifetime. "He works such long hours — fifteen to twenty hours a day," said Peggy McCreary, an engineer who has worked on many of his projects.

At the rate he is going, Prince may prove to be the biggest star of the decade. You can be sure that he'll keep on making hit records, way past the year 1999.

DISCOGRAPHY

ALBUMS BY PRINCE
FOR YOU (1978)
PRINCE (1979)
DIRTY MIND (1980)
CONTROVERSY (1981)
1999 (1982)
PURPLE RAIN (1984)

SELECTED SINGLES
(Prince has released a number of singles with non–LP flip sides)
"1999" b/w "HOW COME U DON'T CALL ME ANYMORE"
"DELIRIOUS" b/w "HORNY TOAD"
"LET'S PRETEND WE'RE MARRIED" b/w "IRRESISTIBLE BITCH"
"WHEN DOVES CRY" b/w "17 DAYS (The rain will come down, then U will have 2 choose. If U believe, look 2 the dawn and U shall never lose.)"
"LET'S GO CRAZY" b/w "EROTIC CITY"
"PURPLE RAIN" b/w "GOD (Love Theme From Purple Rain)"
"I WOULD DIE 4 U" b/w "ANOTHER LONELY CHRISTMAS"

ALBUMS BY THE TIME
THE TIME (1981)
WHAT TIME IS IT? (1982)
ICE CREAM CASTLES (1984)

OTHER ALBUMS PRODUCED BY THE STARR COMPANY
VANITY 6, Vanity 6 (1982)
APOLLONIA 6, Apollonia 6 (1984)
THE GLAMOROUS LIFE, Sheila E. (1984)

(All of these albums and singles are on the Warner Brothers
   label)

ABOUT THE AUTHOR

Gordon Matthews has been living his own version of the rock-and-roll lifestyle for the last ten years. He currently lives in New York City.